Curious Miss Muss

Jan Westberg

Consulting Editor, Diane Craig, M.A./Reading Specialist

ABDO
Publishing Company

Published by ABDO Publishing Company, 4940 Viking Drive, Edina, Minnesota 55435.

Printed in the United States.

Credits
Edited by: Pam Price
Curriculum Coordinator: Nancy Tuminelly
Cover and Interior Design and Production: Mighty Media
Photo and Illustration Credits: BananaStock Ltd., Brand X Pictures, Comstock, Corbis Images, Corel, Digital Vision, Eyewire Images, Hemera, Tracy Kompelien, PhotoDisc, Jan Westberg

Library of Congress Cataloging-in-Publication Data

Westberg, Jan.
    Curious Miss Muss / Jan Westberg.
       p. cm. -- (Rhyme time)
    Includes index.
    ISBN 1-59197-782-7
    1. English language--Rhyme--Juvenile literature. I. Title. II. Rhyme time (ABDO Publishing Company)

PE1517.W475 2004
428.1'3--dc22
                                                                    2004047248

SandCastle™ books are created by a professional team of educators, reading specialists, and content developers around five essential components that include phonemic awareness, phonics, vocabulary, text comprehension, and fluency. All books are written, reviewed, and leveled for guided reading, early intervention reading, and Accelerated Reader® programs and designed for use in shared, guided, and independent reading and writing activities to support a balanced approach to literacy instruction.

Let Us Know

After reading the book, SandCastle would like you to tell us your stories about reading. What is your favorite page? Was there something hard that you needed help with? Share the ups and downs of learning to read. We want to hear from you! To get posted on the ABDO Publishing Company Web site, send us e-mail at:

sandcastle@abdopub.com

SandCastle Level: Fluent

Words that rhyme do
not have to be spelled the
same. These words rhyme
with each other:

bus

hippopotamus

muss

curious

octopus

plus

famous

serious

fuss

us

After school, Ronald waits for the school **bus**.

Cats are known for being curious.

That's a big yawn, even for a hippopotamus!

Aimee and Teresa are practicing a song and dance.

They want to be **famous**.

The **octopus** is hard to see because it blends into its surroundings.

When Jamie has to wear a suit,
he makes a big **fuss**.

Getting ice cream for dessert is always a **plus**.

By the end of the day, Cal's hair is in a **muss**.

Shana asks, "Can you spin
hula hoops like **us**?"

Jennifer is studying the globe.

She looks **serious**.

Curious Miss Muss

An octopus named Miss Muss
was, oh, so very curious
to see if she could be famous.

She called her good friend Gus
the hippopotamus.

Miss Muss had an idea to discuss.

"Gus, I want to be famous,"
said Miss Muss.

Gus said, "If you are
really serious,
then Hollywood is
the place for us."

They got to Hollywood without a fuss.

Miss Muss tried out and was fabulous.
There was a great part for an octopus.

But there was no role for Gus

He was sad and envious.

This was not a plus
for Gus or Miss Muss.

Miss Muss said, "I like you, Gus, more than being famous."

So together they went back home on the bus.

Rhyming Riddle

What do you call a hassle on public transportation?

Bus fuss

Glossary

curious. eager to learn more

envious. the state of both resenting and longing for the property or qualities of another

fuss. a protest or commotion about something, often a trivial matter; a quarrel or fight

hippopotamus. a very large African animal that lives in or near water and has thick skin, short legs, and a wide mouth

Hollywood. a neighborhood in Los Angeles, California, where many movies are made

muss. a mess or an untidy condition

About SandCastle™

A professional team of educators, reading specialists, and content developers created the SandCastle™ series to support young readers as they develop reading skills and strategies and increase their general knowledge. The SandCastle™ series has four levels that correspond to early literacy development in young children. The levels are provided to help teachers and parents select the appropriate books for young readers.

Emerging Readers
(no flags)

Beginning Readers
(1 flag)

Transitional Readers
(2 flags)

Fluent Readers
(3 flags)

These levels are meant only as a guide. All levels are subject to change.

To see a complete list of SandCastle™ books and other nonfiction titles from ABDO Publishing Company, visit www.abdopub.com or contact us at:
4940 Viking Drive, Edina, Minnesota 55435 • 1-800-800-1312 • fax: 1-952-831-1632